BookLife
freedom
Readers

DINO
TREK

BY
SHALINI
VALLEPUR

FOR A
TYRANNOSAURUS
REX

BookLife
PUBLISHING

©2022
BookLife Publishing Ltd.
King's Lynn
Norfolk PE30 4LS

A catalogue record for this
book is available from the
British Library.

ISBN: 978-1-80155-128-1

Written by:
Shalini Vallepur

Edited by:
Madeline Tyler

Designed by:
Jasmine Pointer

BookLife
freedom
Readers

Photocredits:

Images are courtesy of Shutterstock.com.
With thanks to Getty Images, Thinkstock Photo and iStockphoto.

Front Cover - Luis Louro, Herschel Hoffmeyer, alice-photo, topimages, Dimedrol68.
2 - AKKHARAT JARUSILAWONG. 4 - Luis Louro. 5 - paleontologist natural. 6 -
Photomontage. 7 - Elnur. 8 & 9 - Herschel Hoffmeyer. 10 - By Unknown - University
Archives, University of Kansas Library, Public Domain, https://commons.wikimedia.
org/w/index.php?curid=21468325 & ssr ist4u from Ibaraki, Japan [CC BY-SA 2.0 (https://
creativecommons.org/licenses/by-sa/2.0)], via Wikimedia Commons & Lukasz Szwaj, P
Maxwell Photography. 11 - James Kirkikis. 12 - Olena Yakobchuk, Demja. 13 - sunabesyou,
Christian Kornacker. 14 - hans engbers, Bahruz Rzayev. 15 - Marques, CatbirdHill. 16 -
Metha1819, Herschel Hoffmeyer. 17 - JopsStock. 18 - Rattana. 19 - Wlad74,
Ton Bangkeaw. 20 - Ton Bangkeaw. 22 - Henning Marquardt. 23 - Luis Louro.

CONTENTS

WELCOME TO THE DINO-TREK!

Let's go and see some dinosaurs! Are you ready? You will become a palaeontologist and go on an adventure looking for dinosaur fossils.

A palaeontologist is a scientist who studies what life on Earth was like before we humans came around. They go on excavations where they dig up the ground looking for fossils.

WHAT ARE FOSSILS?

A fossil is made when an animal or plant is preserved in rock. The hard parts, such as bone or shell, are left behind. They leave a shape in the rock for us to study. Dinosaur fossils are millions of years old.

Palaeontologists study fossils from animals, plants and bacteria. They treat dinosaur fossils very carefully because they are millions of years old. They use toothpicks and brushes to remove dirt, and magnifying glasses to get a closer look.

TYRANNOSAURUS REX

Tyrannosaurus rex is sometimes called T. rex, and it was a fearsome dinosaur. T. rex had a big tail, large teeth and little arms.

T. rex lived around 68 million years ago. An adult T. rex could grow to six metres tall. If T. rex were around today, it would tower over us!

PALAEONTOLOGISTS
OF THE PAST

BARNUM. BROWN

Palaeontologist Barnum Brown was the first person to find T. rex fossils, in the year 1902. A palaeontologist called Henry Osborn gave the T. rex its name in 1905. It means 'king of tyrant lizards'.

Sue the T. Rex

In 1990, palaeontologist Sue Hendrickson spotted some bones sticking out of a cliff. She excavated the site and discovered a T. rex fossil. The fossil is named after the person who found it – Sue!

LET'S DIG

Now we need to find the right site to start our excavation. We cannot dig under roads and buildings. To find a site, palaeontologists study maps.

We also think about the habitat that T. rex lived in. It is thought that T. rex lived in big, open forests where North America and Mongolia are today.

MONGOLIA

This looks like a T. rex skull. It needs to be carefully taken out of the ground so we can brush off the dirt and get a closer look.

T. REX SKULL

T. REX TOOTH

We can tell what T. rex ate by looking at its teeth. Sharp, pointy teeth are perfect for ripping into meat. This tells us that T. rex was a carnivore and a predator. Some T. rex teeth were 30 centimetres long.

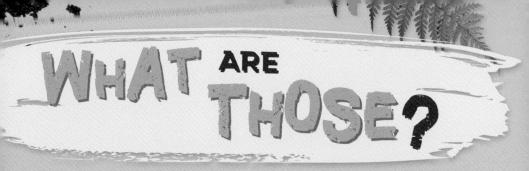

WHAT ARE THOSE?

T. rex was a terrifying, mighty predator with a big body. So why did it have such tiny arms?

Palaeontologists have an explanation for this. They think that T. rex arms were small but very strong. They could attack and slash any prey that came close.

FOLLOW THE FOOTSTEPS

What is that over there? It looks like a dinosaur fossil trackway. These trackways are usually footprints that have been preserved over time. T. rex feet could grow to around one metre, so it's no wonder that it left big footprints behind!

Palaeontologists have found T. rex trackways left by groups of T. rex. They believe that T. rex lived and hunted in groups.

?? WHAT IF... ??

What if T. rex had feathers? It is hard to imagine T. rex as anything but scaly, but palaeontologists are not sure whether T. rex had fabulous feathers or not.

No fossils of T. rex with feathers have been found yet, but fossils cannot always tell us everything. Feathers are soft, so they are less likely to be preserved. For now, we have to guess what T. rex might have looked like with feathers.

THINK AGAIN

Sometimes palaeontologists get things wrong at first. Many believed that T. rex could run very fast to catch prey. Some palaeontologists now say that T. rex was too heavy to run. They think T. rex walked around instead.

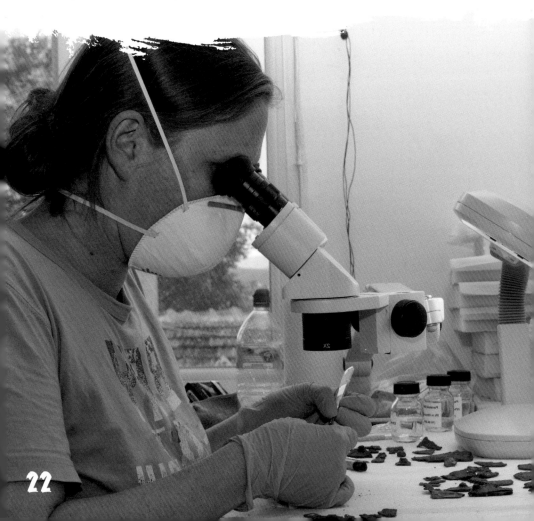

END OF THE TREK

There is still a lot to discover as a palaeontologist. New fossils are being excavated and studied all the time. Maybe one day you could discover a brilliant and fearsome dinosaur like T. rex!

QUESTIONS

1: How tall was T. rex?

2: What was the name of the T. Rex found in 1990?
a) Sue
b) Pugh
c) Barney McGrew

3: How do we know that T. rex ate meat?

4: Why do palaeontologists think T. rex had tiny arms?

5: Do you think T. rex had feathers? Draw what you think a T. rex looked like.

BookLife
freedom
Readers